Contents

D1496644

Lutheran Basics

Writers: Beth Ann Gaede and Margaret Marcrander
Editors: Barbara S. Wilson, Katherine A. Evensen, Virginia Bonde Zarth,
Douglas Schmitz, and Alyn Bedford
Illustrators: Judy Swanson and Jane Pitz
Cover illustrator: Nick Markell

Catechism quotations are from *A Contemporary Translation of
Luther's Small Catechism: Study Edition,* copyright © 1994 Augsburg
Fortress.

Scripture quotations are from New Revised Standard Version Bible,
copyright 1989 Division of Christian Education of the National
Council of the Churches of Christ in the United States of America.
Used by permission.

ISBN 0-8066-3961-X

Manufactured in U.S.A.

Introduction

After three days they found him in the temple, sitting among the teachers, listening to them and asking them questions. LUKE 2:46

We come to church asking questions and seeking answers. Though we sing praises and offer prayers to God in worship, we also seek to know more about the God to whom we sing and pray. In this passage from the Gospel of Luke, Jesus provides a model for all who come through the doors of the church—those who ask, those who learn, and, finally, those who teach.

Like Jesus, you have responded to the promptings of the Spirit. And God promises to meet you where you are, no matter what questions and challenges you bring. Additionally, you bring with you many gifts—your own experiences, knowledge, and feelings as a person of faith. With these gifts you will nurture the faith of other Christians, and in turn find your own faith nurtured.

Lutheran Basics is designed to help you grow in your understanding, appreciation, and practice of the Christian faith. This resource will

- provide you with an outline of the Christian faith as understood by Lutherans;
- help you think and speak with greater confidence about the Christian faith and the Lutheran tradition;
- help you understand, as a person of faith, the unfolding relationship we have with our creating, redeeming, and sanctifying God.

Why Lutheran Theology?

I will meditate on your precepts, and fix my eyes on your ways.
PSALM 119:15

In any relationship of depth we must step back from time to time to evaluate how things are going. So it is in our relationship with God. Theology is the word we speak and live in relation to God. Theology is not faith in the sense of trust; it is our attempt to make sense of God so we learn that God is trustworthy. In stepping back we are able to see how God moves through history, through others, and through ourselves.

The primary source for Lutheran theology is the revelation of God in the person of Jesus Christ as witnessed in scripture. The message throughout the Bible reveals God's passion overwhelming all creation. Furthermore, in scripture we see that God's desire is to be in a loving relationship with us. By reflecting on the biblical stories and themes we come to know God better.

At the heart of the Bible for Lutherans is the witness to Jesus Christ. Christ is the visible revelation of God to us. As we pay attention to what Jesus teaches and his radical act of love for us in the cross and resurrection, we come to understand God as merciful and trustworthy.

But Lutherans also understand scripture as relevant to the way we live our lives. Only after listening to the scriptures can we discern and reflect on our daily walk. For example, if we learn that Jesus is trustworthy, we must ask ourselves if this is truly the God we trust. Or do we have some other god that takes precedence in our lives, such as money, or even our selves?

Our theology allows us to see how we must live faithfully, but it must also issue into a trust-filled relationship with God. Beginning to live it, we come back to study and reflect again.

Lutherans believe that participation in theological reflection
- guides and supports the whole people of God through a lifelong process of faith formation;
- equips believers to proclaim God's grace for all people;
- helps individuals live faithfully in relationship with God, one another, and all creation;
- ensures that the insights from scripture and the confessions that have shaped our faith continue to be passed from one generation to the next.

Grace

For by grace you have been saved through faith, and this is not your own doing; it is the gift of God—not the result of works, so that no one may boast. EPHESIANS 2:8-9

Grace is the love of God, embodied in Jesus Christ, that makes us the holy and beloved people of God. The gospel, or the good news, tells us we do nothing to earn this love. It is absolutely free, on the house, pure gift. "The story of human sin is the story of our rebellion against God. . . . We place ourselves first, before God."[1] In spite of this, God never abandons us. Rather, God embraces us with lavish generosity, conquering death on our behalf and offering us life. In every way, in everything we do, in all we are, God is for us. This is grace.

What Does This Mean?

- God's grace is not a cheap cover-up for our sin. It does more than merely excuse it. Through grace God actually remakes us—we are a new creation.
- We are not forced or obligated to receive God's gift of grace. God gives out of love, and it is God's nature to "grace us," regardless of our response.
- Good works are the fruits of—not payment for—our new, grace-filled relationship with God.

Exploring Scripture

What happens to us because of God's grace?

Romans 5:1-2; 6:1-2
2 Corinthians 5:17-19
2 Thessalonians 2:16-17
2 Timothy 4:8

Looking at Our Experience

- In your own words, what does *grace* mean?
- How does God's grace affect your thoughts and feelings about yourself? other people? the rest of creation? God?
- Do you believe God graces you regardless of how you respond? Why or why not?

---

1. *Evangelical Catechism: Christian Faith in the World Today,* American Edition (Minneapolis: Augsburg Publishing House, 1982), 204.

The Word

Long ago God spoke to our ancestors in many and various ways by the prophets, but in these last days he has spoken to us by a Son. HEBREWS 1:1

We hear God's word in the Bible, and we see God's word in the life, death, and resurrection of Jesus.

From the beginning, God has been determined to communicate with us, to tell us, "This is who I am." God first spoke into the swirling chaos and the world came into being, revealing that our God is a God of order and nurture. Throughout history, God's word has been heard on the lips of people who have reminded us that our God is a God of justice and mercy. And in Jesus we hear God's ultimate word of forgiveness and reconciliation—God's grace for us.

What Does This Mean?

- The words of the Bible point us to the Word, Jesus Christ.
- When we read the Bible, we do more than learn about God. We *meet* God!
- The Bible has authority because Jesus is its center.
- We interpret the Bible within the community of God's faithful, past and present.
- God speaks to us through the Bible not so we may believe *that . . .* , but so we may believe *in* Jesus Christ.

Exploring Scripture

Why did God give us the Bible?
> Psalm 119:105
> Luke 11:28
> Romans 1:16
> 2 Timothy 3:15-17

Looking at Our Experience

- Who gave you your first Bible? Who helped you begin to read the Bible? What was that like?
- What Bible passage most clearly shows you that the center of the Bible is Jesus Christ?
- What difference, if any, has reading the Bible made in your life?

God Creates and Knows Me

I believe in God, the Father almighty, creator of heaven and earth.
(SMALL CATECHISM, FIRST ARTICLE OF THE APOSTLES' CREED)

"In the beginning, God created. . . . And it was very good."

With these words from Genesis 1, the Bible reveals God as creator. Martin Luther tells us in the Small Catechism that creation was not a one-time event. God continues to provide for us and all creation simply out of grace—God's dynamic love for us. We ourselves participate in God's continuing creation by being faithful and loving family members, responsible employees, and imaginative artisans and leaders, and in many other ways.

What Does This Mean?

- We learn about God's faithfulness from God's work in creation.
- We and all things were created "very good."
- God created us to be in relationship—with God, one another, and all creation.
- We also are responsible to care for all creation—our next of kin.

Exploring Scripture

What do these passages tell you about who God is?

Psalm 23:1
Isaiah 64:8
Isaiah 66:13
John 1:1

Looking at Our Experience

- What does it mean to you that God created humanity "very good"?
- How do you care for God's creation?
- What do you see in the world that makes it impossible for you to rely on creation alone to learn about God?
- What difference would it make to you if God were not involved in our world today? How would it be different if God had simply created the world and then left us alone?

Jesus Loves and Saves Me

I believe in Jesus Christ, his only Son, our Lord. (SMALL CATECHISM, SECOND ARTICLE OF THE APOSTLES' CREED)

So passionately does God desire to be in relationship with us that God did the unimaginable: God became one of us.

Jesus Christ, the Son of God, is fully God and fully human. We could also say Jesus is God's grace in the flesh, because we see in Jesus' suffering, death, and resurrection God's total love for us. Through grace—through Jesus—God overcame the power of sin and death so that all creation might be reconciled with God. Belonging to Jesus means "a surrender of whatever it is that keeps us from the ways of God."[1]

What Does This Mean?

- Our relationship with God has been restored by God alone; we are able to contribute nothing.
- "Jesus stands in our place and suffers all that the world and our sins could heap on him, to the point of death."[2]
- We respond to God's work in Jesus by serving him "in eternal righteousness, innocence, and blessedness" (Small Catechism, Apostles' Creed, Explanation of the Second Article).
- We no longer fear death, because Jesus' resurrection shows us that the last word is God's: life.

Exploring Scripture

What images does the Bible use to describe God's work in Jesus?

Isaiah 53:4, 5
John 1:29
1 Corinthians 15:55-57
1 John 3:8

Looking at Our Experience

- Who first told you about Jesus? How did you picture him then?
- When and how has the work of Jesus made a difference to you?
- When you read the Second Article of the Creed, what, if anything, puzzles you?

---

1. Martin E. Marty, *Come and Grow with Us: New Member Basics* (Minneapolis: Augsburg Fortress, 1996), 7.
2. Marty, *Come and Grow with Us: New Member Basics*, 7.

The Holy Spirit Calls and Nurtures Me

I believe in the Holy Spirit . . . (SMALL CATECHISM, THIRD ARTICLE OF THE APOSTLES' CREED)

In his explanation of the Third Article of the Creed, Martin Luther confesses, "I believe that by my own understanding or strength I cannot believe in Jesus Christ my Lord or come to him."

It is God as the Spirit and through the Spirit who enlightens us, makes us holy, and keeps us in faith.[1] In fact, Luther says, the Spirit "calls, gathers, enlightens, and makes holy the whole Christian church on earth" (Small Catechism, Apostles' Creed, Explanation of the Third Article). We see in the Spirit God's grace at work again: Our relationship with God is from beginning to end God's doing, God's love in action.

What Does This Mean?

- Faith, our relationship with God that encompasses every aspect of our being, is entirely a gift from God.
- Faith is not a one-time gift. The Spirit daily nurtures us through word and sacrament and through other believers.
- The church itself is a gift from God, not merely a human institution.

Exploring Scripture

Why do we need the Spirit?

Acts 1:8
1 Corinthians 2:14
1 Peter 2:9
1 John 4:2

Looking at Our Experience

- When have you been most aware of the work of the Holy Spirit?
- How are you different because you have been "made holy"?
- How do you see the Spirit at work in your daily life? your congregation? the church throughout the world?

---

1. Martin E. Marty, *Come and Grow with Us: New Member Basics* (Minneapolis: Augsburg Fortress, 1996), 7.

Worship

"O come, let us worship and bow down, let us kneel before the Lord, our Maker!" PSALM 95:6

Worship is the center of the Christian's life with God.

On Sundays, the day of Jesus' resurrection, and on other festival days throughout the church year, we come together with other Christians to offer God thanks and praise; confess our sins and receive assurance of God's forgiveness; listen to God's word; offer prayers to God; and celebrate the gift of the sacraments, Holy Baptism and Holy Communion. Our worship of God continues when we are sent from the assembly to serve God by serving our neighbor.

What Does This Mean?

- Although we bring our experience, thoughts, and feelings to worship, the focus of worship is God, not people.
- Worship grows out of and reflects God's word, God's self-revelation to us.
- Anything we do to acknowledge God's greatness and love for us—such as serving our neighbor or studying God's word—is in essence an act of worship.

Exploring Scripture

Why do we worship God?
Psalm 95:7
Matthew 28:16-20
John 4:23
Colossians 3:16-17

Looking at Our Experience

- If you were taken to worship when you were a child, what do you remember most clearly?
- Which parts of your congregation's Sunday worship service most nourish you? Why?
- When are you most aware of God's presence during Sunday worship? during the rest of the week?

The Sacraments

But we have this treasure in clay jars, so that it may be made clear that this extraordinary power belongs to God and does not come from us.
2 CORINTHIANS 4:7

Lutherans celebrate two sacraments: Holy Baptism and Holy Communion. The sacraments are another form of God's word, another way God speaks loving words into our ears.

Lutherans teach that a sacrament is a holy or sacred act that (1) imparts God's grace; (2) uses some visible means, such as water or bread and wine; (3) is connected with God's word; and (4) was commanded by Christ. People are made members of the family of God through the sacrament of Holy Baptism, and Christians are sustained for the life of faith through the sacrament of Holy Communion.

What Does This Mean?

- When God wants to reach, no vehicle is too ordinary! Even the "clay jars" of water, bread, and wine are useful to God.
- We call the sacraments "means of grace" because God communicates divine love in and among us through them.
- We "celebrate" the sacraments because to receive faith and forgiveness from God is truly a joy.
- We want to celebrate Holy Communion frequently because we are hungry for God.

Exploring Scripture

What happens when we celebrate the sacraments?

Luke 22:19-20
Acts 8:34-39
1 Corinthians 11:26
Galatians 3:26-27

Looking at Our Experience

- When and where were you baptized? How was this event honored by your family or others?
- What are some ways to remember your baptism?
- When and where did you first participate in Holy Communion? What was that like for you?
- What meaning does Holy Communion have for you now?

Vocation

I [Paul] . . . beg you to lead a life worthy of the calling to which you have been called. EPHESIANS 4:1

Vocation is service to God and one's neighbor.

It is not only pastors and other full-time church workers who are called to a vocation. All Christians can do good work that is blessed by God. One way neighbors, governing authorities, family members, and employers are gifts to us is that in them we find opportunities to serve, to fulfill the call from God that is ours through baptism.

What Does This Mean?

- God is interested in what we do with our time and energy every day, not just on Sunday.
- God does not call us out of the world. We are called to serve God where we do our work—in our daily occupation, family, community, and church.
- A task that serves our neighbor or our world can provide meaning even if it is not interesting or challenging.

Exploring Scripture

What is the purpose of our vocation?

Luke 10:38-42
Ephesians 4:11-13
Colossians 3:20-24
1 Peter 2:9

Looking at Our Experience

- To what vocations have you been called?
- What difference does it make to you if you view an undertaking as vocation, rather than as a job or obligation?
- How does the concept of vocation affect your understanding of your relationship to God? other members of your faith community? coworkers or neighbors? your family? the rest of creation?

Mission

Go therefore and make disciples of all nations, . . . teaching them to obey everything that I have commanded you. MATTHEW 28:19-20

We might be tempted to focus on our own relationship with God, but Jesus was very clear: being a disciple is about making disciples.

We Lutherans call ourselves "evangelical" because "we try to look beyond ourselves to bring the gospel to community life with people of other faiths and those of no faith."[1] Our mission field is wherever there are people who do not know Jesus as Savior. Missionaries are not just other folks who share the gospel on our behalf. We are missionaries because we are Christians.

What Does This Mean?

- Being a Christian is not about having a philosophy to live by or living in a certain way. It is about passing on God's gift.[2]
- If we know someone who does not know Jesus, we have a mission to accomplish.
- If we do not know anyone who does not know Jesus, we still have a mission to accomplish!

Exploring Scripture

What message do we teach to all nations?

Luke 4:18-19
Acts 10:34-43
1 Corinthians 15:3-4
Ephesians 2:17-22

Looking at Our Experience

- Who has brought God's word to you? How?
- How do you feel when you think about sharing the gospel with someone?
- What gifts has God given you for your mission work?
- Whom do you know who needs to hear the good news? How could you begin telling that person about Jesus?

---

1. Martin E. Marty, *Come and Grow with Us: New Member Basics* (Minneapolis: Augsburg Fortress, 1996), 29.
2. Marty, *Come and Grow with Us: New Member Basics,* 29.

Law and Gospel

For God so loved the world that he gave his only Son, so that everyone who believes in him may not perish but may have eternal life. JOHN 3:16

Law represents the demands of God, and the gospel is the promises of God.[1]

We encounter God's word as both law and gospel, and we need to hear both. Without the law, we do not know we need the gospel. Without the gospel, the law can only kill. God uses the law in two ways: to keep good order in creation and to drive sinful humans to depend on God alone. God offers the gospel to us, restoring our relationship with God.

What Does This Mean?

- The law is a gift from God, because it shows us clearly that we cannot be right with God through our own effort.
- The gospel does not lessen the demands of the law, but it gives us the heart to do freely what the law requires.
- We do good works not to earn God's favor but to serve our neighbor. We respond with good works because God loves us.

Exploring Scripture

How does the Bible characterize the law?

Deuteronomy 4:5-8
Psalm 119:105-112
Matthew 5:17-18
Galatians 2:16

Looking at Our Experience

- When did someone's "laying down the law" turn out to be a good thing for you?
- Do you think it is a good idea to preach only the gospel and not the law? Why or why not?
- Of which are you usually more aware in your life—the law or the gospel?
- What does it mean to you that the gospel makes you "free"?

---

1. Martin E. Marty, *Come and Grow with Us: New Member Basics* (Minneapolis: Augsburg Fortress, 1996), 10.

Saints and Sinners

I do not understand my own actions. For I do not do what I want, but I do the very thing I hate. ROMANS 7:15

Although we are members of the "community of saints," we are still sinners.

Every day we face the conflict that "*daily* the old person in us with all our sins and evil desires is to be drowned through sorrow for sin and repentance, and that *daily* a new person is to come forth and rise up to live before God in righteousness and purity forever" (emphasis added, Small Catechism, Explanation of the Sacrament of Holy Baptism). We are not sometimes sinners and sometimes saints. We are always *both* saints and sinners.

What Does This Mean?

- When we say we are sinners, we are talking about our human *condition,* not only about our individual deeds.
- The Bible does not distinguish large sins from small ones. "All have sinned and fall short of the glory of God" (Romans 3:23).
- Our dilemma will be resolved only at the end of time, when the reign of God is brought to fulfillment.

Exploring Scripture

What does the Bible say about our condition as saints and sinners?
John 8:34-36
Acts 10:43
Colossians 1:13-14
1 John 1:8-9

Looking at Our Experience

- What does it mean to you that you are a sinner? a saint?
- What might you say to a person who believes humans are naturally good?
- If you could choose to be a saint, would you? Why or why not?

Two Kingdoms

For our struggle is not against enemies of blood and flesh, but against . . . the cosmic powers of this present darkness. EPHESIANS 6:12

As God's faithful people, we live in "two kingdoms."

God speaks to the civil order (or everything "secular") through the law and to the church through the gospel. The law tells us we need to have regard for our neighbor's welfare. The gospel brings grace to the sinner who serves the neighbor only imperfectly. The civil order is established by and responsible to God, although it is not specifically Christian.[1]

What Does This Mean?

- God rules, although in different ways, over both the kingdom of the world and the kingdom of God.
- The kingdom of the world is finite, necessary for sustaining daily life, and good.
- The kingdom of God is eternal and is concerned with faith and salvation.
- Christians can be responsible citizens, both opposing evil and loving their neighbor.

Exploring Scripture

What does the Bible say about the Christian's relationship to the civil order?

John 15:18-25
Romans 13:1-7
Colossians 1:16
1 Peter 2:13-17

Looking at Our Experience

- When have you felt a conflict between your civil responsibilities and your life as a Christian?
- Have you ever spoken out against an injustice in the world? Why or why not?
- What do you think and how do you feel when the church gets involved in politics? Why?

---

1. Martin E. Marty, *The Lutheran People* (Royal Oak, Mich.: Cathedral Publishers, 1973), 30-31.

A Lutheran Vocabulary

absolution: the forgiveness of our sins in the name of Jesus

atonement: the work of Jesus to restore our relationship with God

church: all who have been called by the Holy Spirit and belong to Christ; the body of Christ

confession of sins: acknowledging before God our sins against God in thought, word, and deed

creed: a statement of belief, especially one of the three historic statements of the Christian faith (Apostles', Nicene, Athanasian)

disciple: one chosen by God to follow Jesus and share the gospel with others

faith: a relationship with God based on trust in God's saving promise

gospel: the good news of salvation through Jesus; one of the first four books of the New Testament

grace: God's gift of love and forgiveness freely given to undeserving sinners

justification: God's declaration that our relationship with God has been made right because of the work of Jesus

reconciliation: God's action through Jesus to restore our relationship with God and our neighbor

repentance: turning from sin; feeling sorry for our sins and resolving to change

sacrament: an act that imparts God's grace, it uses visible means, is connected with the word of God, and is commanded by Christ; for Lutherans, Holy Baptism and Holy Communion

salvation: God's work to rescue us from the consequences of our sin, so that we might live in restored relationships on this earth and eternally

sanctification: the work of the Holy Spirit to call us daily to new life in Christ

sin: self-centeredness; placing self in God's place, resulting in total alienation from God

Trinity: the doctrine reflecting God's revelation that God is three persons—Father, Son, and Holy Spirit—who are fully God and eternal

word of God: God's revelation to us through the person of Jesus Christ and through the Bible, which points us to Jesus

worship: God's people coming together to acknowledge God with praise and thanks